SHOULDS! DON'T COUNT

Life in a Nutshell, Positive Choice vs. Negative Choice, and a Year without a Should

[handwritten signature inscription]

D. C. Williams

BALBOA.
PRESS
A DIVISION OF HAY HOUSE

Author Credits:
65 YEARS OF LIFE'S LESSONS

Balboa Press books may be ordered through booksellers or by contacting:

Balboa Press
A Division of Hay House
1663 Liberty Drive
Bloomington, IN 47403
www.balboapress.com
1 (877) 407-4847

Because of the dynamic nature of the Internet, any web addresses or links contained in this book may have changed since publication and may no longer be valid. The views expressed in this work are solely those of the author and do not necessarily reflect the views of the publisher, and the publisher hereby disclaims any responsibility for them.

The author of this book does not dispense medical advice or prescribe the use of any technique as a form of treatment for physical, emotional, or medical problems without the advice of a physician, either directly or indirectly. The intent of the author is only to offer information of a general nature to help you in your quest for emotional and spiritual well-being. In the event you use any of the information in this book for yourself, which is your constitutional right, the author and the publisher assume no responsibility for your actions.

Any people depicted in stock imagery provided by Thinkstock are models, and such images are being used for illustrative purposes only.
Certain stock imagery © Thinkstock.

Printed in the United States of America.

ISBN: 978-1-4525-2160-2 (sc)
ISBN: 978-1-4525-2162-6 (hc)
ISBN: 978-1-4525-2161-9 (e)

Library of Congress Control Number: 2014915923

Balboa Press rev. date: 09/18/2014

Dedication

To my paternal grandfather George (Tata) Cisneros and my mother Christine Telles, Cisneros, Estrella.

TATA was wise beyond his formal education. He believed in the power of the individual. His favorite saying was, "The World is destined for Greatness, be a part of it"!

Mother, (Grandma Chris), managed, as a divorced mother of three, to raise my brother, sister and me to be responsible adults, by reminding us that "Shoulds! Don't Count."

They both had a benevolent Spirit worthy of the love they gave and they received. They taught LOVE as their first language.

Contents

Preface

The writing of this book began in March, 1984. The Story of its beginning is the Introduction.

Not until 2006, did I realize the lessons I received have been a guide to personal responsibility as taught by all the great teachers throughout my life time and before. Nothing is new or unusual. GOD made the lessons simple and clear. We as a mass make it difficult. Observe, in these simple windows examples of the HAD, HAVE and Should in our Lives.

Whether you are 8 years or 100 years old, Life is now!

Whether we are here tomorrow doesn't matter. Only this moment counts.

How we live now, today, is our choice and our legacy. Our choices create good or negative results in our life.

This rendering is not for the faint of Heart.

Since you are reading this book, you are obviously "Left Behind" as it were. We are forever in an internal battle between Good (positive) and Retrograde Mind Set (negative) energy. .

GOOD: Peace of mind & spirit "With Malice, Toward None." A Healthy, Wealthy, Wise and Happy Life with Balance and Peace of Mind as an overall Goal in Life.

EVIL/Retrograde Activity: Using one's Free Will and choosing to live a life of hate, violence, revenge, and turmoil by trying to destroy all that is good and beautiful within us and around us. Promoting imbalance and turmoil in one's life. Disrupting ones peace of mind

Finding out that we alone are in control of the way we act, feel, and respond to whatever choice or adversity GOD has given us, is not an easy task. Our life is tracked by our Had's, Have's, Did, and Didn't Do. "Shoulds, Don't Count!"

* FEAR, HATE AND ANGER ARE KNOWN TO CAUSE MANY

ILLNESSES AND PROMOTE EVIL DEEDS THROUGHOUT THE WORLD.

* LOVE AND FORGIVENESS ARE KNOWN TO CURE ILLNESS AND PREVENT RETROGRADE DEEDS

My Grandfather was 64 years old, weighed 325 pounds, was an Orange Picker Supervisor, the father of 8 and a Senior Deacon of his Church. When he passed away there were hundreds of people at his memorial service. He mattered! He left a legacy of Good. He loved his GOD, his family, himself and his fellow man. He died a good and simple man, with "Malice toward None." He is at peace, as are the majority of people who knew him.

Evil Doers (Retrograde perpetrators) leave emptiness and casualties behind. They are without peace in their life, or in their death. Their connection with a natural positive Life has been severed. Turmoil is all they create and all they leave behind for those who loved them and thought they knew them. Peace is lost for Spirits such as these.

Humans need to be taught tenderness and love as children in order for the positive power of goodness of Free Will to prevail over the negative Free Will choices in life. I was blessed, at birth, with positive energy which has seen me through many emotional valleys and near death instances. This positive base allowed me to understand and support others through their growth and pain.

The lessons I've received over the years were taught whenever I ignored or discounted my own internal warning system. Some people might call it our "inner voice". My proverbial inner voice would loudly say "NO" or "Don't Go". As a teenager I ignored the clear warning not to go. In defiance of my step father who also said," don't go"! I went with my friends and got into a car accident at age 16.

The accident caused a head injury and temporary paralysis on my right side. I recovered, except for the loss of a precious and valuable gift. My photo graphic memory was gone. Before the accident, I could recall any thing I had seen or read. A clear picture would appear and allow me to read the article or passage verbatim or see the image as if it were sitting in front of me. The car accident caused me to lose one precious gift and acquire another. The subsequent Gift is the realization that life is precious and to be lived, loved and honored. At age 19, I back packed Europe, at 21 I back packed the Hawaiian Islands of Kauai, Maui, and Oahu. The rest of my life has been viewed through the eyes of gratitude and love for all that is precious on our planet.

LOVE of all living things is the true key to, "Peace on Earth, as well as it is in Heaven". This is Clarity with or without monetization! Very few, manage to reach such a state. There are many who embrace Love as a way of life and are blessed with peace of mind and sometimes ridiculed as being weak and naive for their compassion. These people know that they know and "keep on, keeping on." "With Malice toward none" and reverence for the whole of humanity.

The Circle of life is best served when our physical life on Earth is ended without a casualty left behind or a should on ones last breath. Wars create, and are, a man made should for humanity. Natural disasters create shoulds for those left behind. Death through bad health and medical issues are results of shoulds come and gone. A clear spirit can cure disease, enhance one's life expectancy and secure Peace of Mind. Planning is a great way to prepare yourself for coping, forgiving all, including yourself makes for a better exit and better state for a next level, if you believe there is one. Aloha, is from our benevolent God! Whatever you wish to call the IAM.

Love of mankind is a worthy lesson. Jesus taught it! Mohandas Gandhi taught it! Buddha taught it! Mohammad taught it! Moses taught it! Abraham Lincoln taught it! Mother Teresa taught it! Martin Luther King taught it! John Lennon taught it! Princess Diana taught it! John F. Kennedy taught it! Nelson Mandela taught it! Maya Angelou taught it. GOD, the overall power of the Universe, promotes it!

Masters teach it, **others** strive to **embrace it,** and **takers** strive to **destroy it**!

GOD made it simple and easy. The purpose of this book is to help survivors remember the positive lessons, choose well and strive to eliminate the negative should in their lives.

GOD keeps sending us messages and some see. GOD will keep sending messages for you and for me.

Acknowledgement

In 1980, a wonderful group of people allowed me to stay with them, on the beautiful Island of Kauai, during a very difficult time in my life. A traumatic divorce triggered painful emotions which I had accumulated over the years. Apparently, I was very good at hiding and controlling these emotions up until that time. The personal poems noted here are the unraveling and healing of those issues allowing me to obtain some clarity once more in my life.

Mahalo! Thank You! Gracias! Domo Arigato! Danka! To Sheryl Holland Holt-Keliipio, her husband Alex, daughter Kalei, and son Ryan. Their friends Colleen Witt-Han, her husband Presley and their two young daughters were all very thoughtful and supportive.

KODO's! To Rene Yamashiro, Margaret Case, Betty Parker, Bill Kruse and my niece Jerri Lynn Hewitt Aminikharrazi for honoring me by thinking of Had's.

Special Thanks to: Mary M. Harkins, Grace Darling-Hunter, Florence Cigi-Williams, Iris Chang-Dawson, Kathy Taira & Charlie, Carolyn Moss Steiner-Frank, Teresa Hamilton, Betty Koslow, Georgiana May, Sherrill Franklin, Sue Carson-Hubert, my niece Kelly Hewitt, and a very wise friend Tina Kalmutzki, for providing me with discussion, support and profound life lessons. Without their support, this would never have been completed.

The true GOD of Love, is My GOD, is
Your GOD, and is Their GOD!!

LIFE'S CHOICES!

SHOULDLESS   FULL OF SHOULD

FREE WILL

**THE PROVERBIAL
NUT SHELL!**

LIFE IN A NUTSHELL!   SHOULD'S DON'T COUNT!

Introduction

This book is an anomaly

One day in March 1984 at 2am in the morning I was compelled to wake up and write most of the personal poems in this book. Not until 20 years later did my writings become relevant.

I was living on the island of Oahu in Hawaii, one of the most beautiful locations on Earth as well as the farthest west one can travel and still be in the United States. Hawaii is so far west its East. Nowhere else in America will you find a magnificent culmination of humanity at its best? This small chain of islands attracts people from every part of the world and for the most part they get along in a civil adult manner.

I attribute the ability of these people to get along well, to the Hawaiian born American: Japanese, Chinese, Samoan, Tongan, Pilipino, German, French, Indian, Hispanic, Mexican, British, Canadian, Portuguese and every combination of American found there. Locals introduce their friends and acquaintances to their children as Auntie or Uncle. "There are no strangers only friends they haven't met yet."

Our world today is at a place in time where our free will is being challenged. Not by armies but by the Choices we are given, the Choices we have made, and the Choices yet to be made. Which will the Human Race Choose, "A Positive path" or "A Negative Path" for our lives?

Hawaii is a microcosm of the World. The Good go there to enjoy the natural beauty of God, which has been created for us here on Earth. Those who have made bad decisions go there to hide from something or someone. The beauty is easily found by those who come looking for it, but is illusive to those who are using it as a cloak.

As in all places on Earth people exercise their free will. The Aloha Spirit offered there is free and clear when you have lived a life with positive Hads. If you are trying to get away from your negative Hads you will find that you brought them with you. Opportunity for change is here.

Life in a Nutshell:

The following three words and their definitions are just another example of the power of three which directs, archives, and control our choices in life. They are, "Life in a Nutshell".

HAD:

Past tense of have, here and gone….Has Been, a PERSON LONG PAST HIS HAD…Has…3rd singular presence indicative of the verb have.

HAVE:

Something to work for and obtain…Something that is yours to hold and possess at any moment "PEACE OF MIND"

SHOULD:

Auxiliary verb, past participle of shall…Future in the past tense of verbs with Pronouns I or WE. Auxiliary used after the words expressing… Opinion, obligation, Intention, desire, and probability…The by- product of procrastination / "Manana"!

This rendering is an Ode to Choices made and Choices yet to be made. The simple basic of life is our Free Will sphere with "Life in a Nut Shell". Our task on this Planet is to **Acknowledge the HAD, Eliminate the**

SHOULD, and Rejoice in our Have, in order to establish Peace of Mind, in our Life Time.

Grace and Gratitude expressed by and toward all on Earth promotes Peace and Love!

Mother said, "Shoulds, Don't Count!"

CHAPTER 1

The Way Of Had

HAD, is an ancient three letter word whose importance has gone unacknowledged for far too long. Ages have gone by since the very first Had was initiated, "Had to Create Life."

From that point on Life has been and endless chain of "Had".

Our very Human experience begins with "Had to breathe" and end with "Had to stop breathing." Between our first breath and our last breath, there are Hads, Haves and Should.

Mankind is our Hads. Every Had created throughout history is a link to the Have we experience today. Psychologists say, "Humans learn by repetition and emotional involvement", yet we keep repeating the lessons and learn very slowly.

We as a mass still allow the one individual with a warped sense of negative purpose to influence the way we interact with each other. We live in the He, She, It, They, You and I should way.

The true way, is living in "The Truth and the light" with purpose and positive respect for one another. Not as lemmings, but as individuals in an intricate tapestry of unique beings. As residents of Planet Earth, living a positive life is our task.

The Had is a way we track the existence of all who were. The more famous and provocative the Individual, the more memorable the Hads.

1

ANCIENT HADS:

JESUS… HAD A PURPOSE

MOHAMMED…HAD HIS RULES

ATILLA THE HUN…HAD BAD BREATH

HAMLET…HAD TO BORROW EARS

JOAN OF ARCH…HAD A CAUSE

GHANGIS KHAN…HAD HIS ARMIES

MOSES…HAD A MISSION

QUEEN ELIZABETH I…HAD POWER

SPARTANS…HAD STYLE & UNITY

KING ARTHUR…HAD MERLIN

CLEOPATRA…HAD AN ASP

KING KAMAHAMAHA…HAD THE POWER TO UNITE

MONA LISA…HAD A SMIRK

BUDDHA…HAD WISDOM

ALADDIN…HAD A LAMP

ALI BABA…HAD 40 THIEVES

BEN HUR'S MOTHER…HAD LEPROSY, IT WENT AWAY

POMPEII…HAD ITS LAST DAY

LAWRENCE...HAD AN ADVENTURE IN ARABIA

THE CHINESE...HAD THE WALL

THE VIKINGS...HAD THOR

ROBIN HOOD...HAD HIS MERRY MEN

TIBET...HAD THE DALI LAMA

JAPAN...HAD THE SAMURAI

HONOLULU...HAD PEARL HARBOR

THE EARTH...HAD TO EVOLVE

DINOSAURS...HAD THEIR MOMENT

ANCIENT ALIENS...HAD THEIR VISIT

OUTER-SPACE...HAD LEGENDS

THE SPHINX...HAD BUILDERS

MAYANS...HAD A CALENDAR

CONFUSCIOUS...HAD A SAYING

CHINA...HAD POTENTIAL

SAMURAI...HAD HONOR

INDIA...HAD GANDHI

ABRAHAM LINCOLN...HAD THE GETTYSBURG ADDRESS

LEONARDO D'VINCI...HAD DESIRE/PASSION

3

CHISTOPHER COLUMBUS...HAD THREE BOATS

HANNIBAL...HAD ELEPHANTS

JULES VERN...HAD A GREAT IMAGINATION

CAPTAIN COOK...HAD A BAD TRIP

GREEKS...HAD THEIR TRADITIONS

KNIGHTS TEMPLAR...HAD A SECRET TASK

AMERICAN INDIANS...HAD THEIR PIPE

AFRICA...HAD ITS BEGINNING

EGYPT...HAD THE PHARAOHS

MAID MARIAN...HAD STRENGTH

IRELAND...HAD LEPRCHAUN

ENGLAND...HAD STONE HENDGE

MEXICO...HAD PANCHO VIA

PERU...HAD VISITORS; AUSTRALIA...HAD THE
ABORIGINES,

WHAT ANCIENT HADS DO YOU REMEMBER?

MOST THINGS BUILT ON STRONG FOUNDATIONS OR
PRINCIPLES PREVAIL AND EXIST TODAY!

WELL KNOWN HADS:

EINSTEIN...HAD A THEORY

ALEXANDER BELL...HAD A HEARING AID

DOCTOR SALK...HAD A CURE FOR POLIO

LOUIS ARMSTRONG...HAD LIPS

DWIGHT D EISENHOWER...HAD GOLF CLUBS

GEORGE PATTON...HAD PEARL HANDLED GUNS

BUTCH CASSIDY...HAD THE SUNDANCE KID

MAHANDAS GHANDHI...HAD A WEIGHT PROBLEM

ADOLF HITLER...HAD A MOUSTACHE

JIMMY DURANTE...HAD A NOSE

BETTE DAVIS...HAD EYES

RICHARD NIXON...HAD TAPES

FARAH FAWCETT...HAD GREAT TEETH

LYNDON JOHNSON...HAD LADY BIRD

ZAZA GABOR...HAD HER HUSBANDS

ALFALFA...HAD A COWLICK

NUCLEAR FISSION...HAD ITS DEBUT,

TOM SELLICK...HAD A CHANCE! BUT DIDN'T CALL ME BACK

MOUNT SAINT HELENS...HAD TO BLOW

WONDER WOMAN...HAD A LASSO OF TRUTH

BATMAN...HAD OUR BACK

ABRAHAM LINCOLN...HAD EYES TO SEE GLORY

MICKEY ROONEY... HAD LIFTS

JOHNNY CARSON---HAD HIS WIVES

SUPERMAN...HAD HIS STRENGTH

DISNEY...HAD LAND & VISION

ALFRED NEWMEN...HAD HIS MAD MAG

BEATLES...HAD THEIR FANS

NEW YORK CITY...HAD ITS DEBT,

VIETNAM...HAD ITS WASTE

VIDEO...HAD PACMAN

ALEX HALEY...HAD ROOTS

MAE WEST...HAD MAJOR AFFAIRS

OPRAH...HAD A GIFT

DALLAS...HAD J R

THE KENNEDY'S...HAD THEIR MOMENT

HONOLULU...HAD HAD ITS HURRICANE

SNOOPY...HAD THE RED BARON

PRINCESS GRACE...HAD A TRAGIC ENDING

PRINCESS DIANA...HAD THE LOVE OF THE WORLD

PETER PAN...HAD NEVERLAND

CINDERELLA...HAD HER PRINCE

GRUCHO MARX...HAD A CIGAR

HIAWATHA...HAD A BOW AND ARROW

SLEEPING BEAUTY...HAD HER DWARFS

BRIAR RABBIT...HAD THE BRIAR PATCH

BETTY GRABLE...HAD LEGS

GILLIGAN...HAD AN ISLAND

GARFIELD THE CAT...HAD HIS DOG ODIE

DARTH VADER...HAD SECOND THOUGHTS

MASH...HAD ITS FINALE

ET...HAD US FEELING

SPACE SHIP ENTERPRIZE...HAD A MISSION

HARRY TRUMAN...HAD THE ATOM BOMB

JIMMY CARTER...HAD FRECKLES

SONYA HEINE...HAD SKATES

ESTHER WILLIAMS…HAD TO SWIM

MARK SPITZ…HAD SPEEDOS

ROD STEWART…HAD PASSION

BOY GEORGE…HAD MAKE-UP

RONALD REAGAN…HAD TRICKLE DOWN ECONOMICS

IHATOLLA KOMEINI…HAD HIS TURBAN ON TOO TIGHT

MR.T HAD GOLD

GOLDA MEIR…HAD HER PLACE IN TIME

KEANU REEVES…HAD A CALLING

SYLVESTER STALLONE…HAD A BRAINSTORM

HOWARD HUGHES…HAD A BIZARRE LIFE

PRINCE PHILLIP…HAD HIS WAY

BILL CLINTON…HAD A CHANCE

GEORGE W BUSH… HAD A CHOICE

ROBERT REDFORD…HAD MY HEART

YODA…HAD AMAZING POWERS

TOM CRUISE…HAD A WONDERFUL CAREER

NICOLE KIDMAN…HAD MANY OPTIONS

ROBIN WILLIAMS...HAD IT ALL BUT, DIDN'T FEEL OUR LOVE

GOLDIE HAWN...HAD AN OPEN SPIRIT

ELIZABETH TAYLOR...HAD REAL BEAUTY

WARREN BETTY...HAD A POLITICAL BENT

MICHAEL JACKSON...HAD A HUGE CAREER

HALEY BERRY...HAD BOND

RIYHANA...HAD AN ANGRY BOYFRIEND

MENENDEZ BROTHERS...HAD PARENT ISSUES

THE TITANIC...HAD A VOYAGE

MOUNT RUSHMORE...HAD A FATHER

STEVE JOBS ...HAD TO CREATE APPLE

SHIRLEY MCLAINE...HAD PANACHE

MARY HARKINS...HAD HER POEMS

CHRISTINE TELLES...HAD HER CHILDREN

STEVEN SPIELBERG...HAD STORIES TO TELL

MOTHER TERESA...HAD HER PATH

HE, SHE, IT AND THEY... HAD CHOICES

MICHAEL J. FOX...HAD A GREAT CAREER

JAIMIE FOX...HAD HIS GRAND MOTHER

REDD FOX...HAD NASTY JOKES

ALAN ALDA...HAD A GREAT VOICE

JANE FONDA...HAD LESSONS TO LEARN

LEONARDO DI'CAPRIO...HAD NOMINATIONS

AUNT BERT...HAD HER WAYS

AUNT PATSY...HAD UNCLE DON

UNCLE SAM...HAD MY VOTE

FARANTE...HAD TAISHER

RUSH LIMBAUGH...HAD HIS WIND

FIDEL CASTRO...HAD CUBA

MARTHA STEWART...HAD A VACATION

JOHN LENNON...HAD YOKO ONO

ANDY WILLIAMS...HAD SAN FRANCISCO

JERRY LEWIS...HAD HUTSPUH

JOAN RIVERS...HAD A MOUTH

JAY LENO...HAD MINIS & CYCLES

COLIN POWELL...HAD PERSONAL POWER

BERT...HAD ERNIE

OSAMA BIN LADEN…HAD SHOULDS

UNCLE TED…HAD AUNT DOROTHY

BARAK H. OBAMA…HAD HIS SAY, MICHAEL

JORDAN…HAD HIS PLAY

WILL SMITH…HAD PRESENCE

OPRAH WINFREY…HAD HER OWN INSPIRATION

TOM HANKS…HAD STRENGTH & DEPTH

ELTON JOHN…HAD MAGIC MUSIC

DAVID LETTERMAN…HAD HIS LIST

ANNA NICOLE SMITH…HAD IT ALL WRONG

SANDRA BULLOCK…HAD DEPTH & CHARACTER

MONIQUE…HAD POWER

MICHELLE OBAMA…HAD HER GIRLS

QUEEN LATIFA…HAD UNLIMITED TALENT

TOM AMINIKHARRAZI…HAD JERRI LYNN

KELLYHEWITT…HAD FAITH

ZACK B. WILLIAMS…HAD GOD'S BLESSING

JAMES CAMERON…HAD TITANIC & AVATAR

SEAN CONNERY…HAD STYLE & M

DIANE KEATING...HAD THE VISION

PAUL MCCARTNEY...HAD A WONDEROUS GIFT

SUSAN SARANDON...HAD THELMA & LOUISE

NEIL DIAMOND... HAD DEPTH AND CHARM

GOOGLE...HAD MARKET SHARE

MEL GIBSON...HAD THE PASSION

BARBARA STREISAND...HAD THE VOICE

TINA KALMUTSKI...HAD MICHAEL

SAM WALTON...HAD MARKET SHARE

BERNIE MADOFF...HAD THE NERVE

WILLARD WILLIAMS...HAD STRENGTH OF LOVE

JACK NICOLAS...HAD THE SMIRK

KATHY TAIRA...HAD ROSSY

DONALD TRUMP...HAD 4 BANKRUPTSIES

WHOOPIE GOLDBERG...HAD HUTSPAH

MAN... HAD FREE WILL

WARREN BUFFET...HAD A MORAL COMPASS

ELVIS PRESLEY...HAD HIPS

NELSON MANDELA...HAD TRUTH

MAYA ANGELOU...HAD GRACE AND WISDOM

BILL AND MELINDA GATES... HAD BALANCE

GIVERS...HAD AND HAVE A MANDATE FROM GOD TO PROMOTE GOODNESS

TAKERS...HAD AN OPPORTUNITY AND CHOSE TO DISCONNECT FROM LOVE

NELSON MANDELA...HAD A LOVING SPIRIT AND LOVE FOR HIS FELLOW MAN

I...HAD BELIEF; IT IS NEVER TOO LATE TO START LISTENING TO YOUR INNER

VOICE.

UNIVERSAL HADS:

Had to Breathe... Had Freckles... Had to cry

Had no fear...Had gas...Had to climb

Had to wet...Had a broken arm...Had a bottle

Had a bike...Had a mommy...Had a nap

Had to have it...Had a nap...Had a Minister

Had an Amman...Had a Monk...Had cold

Had a Priest...Had a Guru...Had a Rabbi

Had to burp...Had bronzed shoes...Had a diaper

Had a portrait…Had a point…Had a rash

Had to hide…Had DADA…Had a ponytail

Had to laugh…Had to tell…Had to meditate

Had a pacifier…Had skates…Had a fever

Had a skateboard…Had to let Live…Had a cold

Had a sled…Had no teeth…Had Grandpa

Had a nanny…Had Grandma

Had measles…Had marbles…Had chicken pox

Had a tricycle…Had to sleep…Had to ask

Had a vision…Had a friend…Had to play

Had a wagon…Had to crawl…Had to swim

Had the Flu…Had a brother…Had a puppy

Had a sister…Had a cut…Had a guppy

Had a Room…Had teeth…Had bedtime

Had candy…Had to walk…Had a hamster

Had to grow…Had a puppy…Had popcorn

Had peanut butter…Had a cavity…Had to spit

Had a toothache…Had braces…Had disease

Had tap shoes…Had a yoyo…Had ballet shoes

Had fun...Had boxing gloves...Had fear

Had a messy room...Had a pony...Had a baton

Had a TV...Had an orthodontist...Had a bike

Had Dad's attention...Had Mom's support...Had a sailor Suit

Had two left feet...Had a punishment...Had baby fat

Had time out...Had pride...Had a question

Had a catcher's mask...Had a dentist...Had a pediatrician

Had a secret...Had a place...Had to grow

Had counseling...Had to pout...Had a temper tantrum

Had Pride...Had a video game...Had imaginary friends...Had nightmares

Had Holidays...Had a goat...Had catechism

Had Church on Sunday...Had daycare...Had a babysitter

Had no patience...Had a need...Had a great smile

Had a blessing from GOD...Had a party...Had no reason to hate

Had every reason to live...Had a piñata...Had a siesta

Had to cry...Had to apologize... Had to go to my room

Had to say I am Sorry... Had to share... Had undo it

Had to sell lemonade...Had to ride a bike...Had to pick oranges

Had to hunt for food…Had to trust adults…Had to be cared for

Had every right to be loved…Had every question…Had a slumber party

Had pajamas…Had slippers…Had a teddy bear

Had a slip n slide….Had overalls…Had a slide

Had a good teacher…Had straight A's…Had a spelling bee

Had an excuse for everything… Had a Temple…Had hormones

Had a wart…Had fun…Had a party…Had questions…Had wrong answers

Had to dance…Had a mom…Had a Zit…Had a snack

Had a curfew…Had funds…Had cramps…Had to do the dishes

Had to make the bed…Had to clean the room…Had to take a bath

Had chores…Had a Dog…Had to take a bath

Had a friend…Had a hotdog…Had a coke…Had no right

Had to sing…Had every right…Had to revive

Had New wave…Had punk music…Had to cheer

Had a woody…Had a period…Had to cruise…Had pets

Had no boundaries…Had nerve…Had to dump the trash

Had to crush…Had an excuse…Had a reason

Had to keep going…Had a malt…Had to play video games

Had a sun burn…Had to act…Had the gang

Had an itch…Had a girlfriend…Had a boyfriend

Had a blast…Had a problem…Had a car

Had an excuse…Had curiosity…Had energy…Had gum

Had to talk…Had to amuse…Had to cry…Had breasts

Had to laugh…Had to graduate…Had to believe…

Had to teach… Had to learn…Had to go…Had to joke…Had to call

Had an endless summer…Had spring break…Had winter holidays

Had to joy ride…Had to rebel…Had to apologize

Had to be shown…Had to be told…Had to follow

Had a thought…Had to explore…Had to ignore

Had hair…Had to play music…Had rock music…Had a Nana

Had an image…Had a secret…Had Friends…

Had fears…Had confusion at 13…Had hope…Had puppy love

Had to change…Had a positive spirit…Had to run

Had full range…Had discipline…Had vision…Had joy

Had an idea…Had remorse…Had Choices…Had an iPod…Had Light

Had no clue…Had a routine…Had Love…Had doubts…Had tea… Had rice… Had hope…

Had a deadline…Had anticipation…Had the final word…Had Trust…Had Love…

HAD A PROBLEM, HAD AN ARGUMENT, HAD A CHOICE!
STOP! STOP THIS MADNESS!
YOU'RE ADULTS! YOU CAN REASON WITH EACH OTHER WORK THINGS OUT!
WELL
ALL RIGHT! I WILL IF HE WILL!
SURE, I'LL GIVE IT A TRY!
WONDERFUL.
NOW, HOW DID THIS ALL START
HE HIT ME FIRST
HE SHOULD, YOU SHOULD, THEY DIED!!

MY LIST OF HAD:

Had...a Childhood in Southern California

Had...grandparents...George & Naomi Cisneros...Alfredo & Amelia Telles

Had...a father and mother...Edward R Cisneros & Christine Telles

Had...a darling step-sister (Laura) who passed away with measles encephalitis at age 5.

Had...a weight problem most of my life

Had...a car accident age 16

Had...a second chance at life

Had...the opportunity to travel Europe & Hawaii

Had...18 Years promoting Physical Therapy in California & Hawaii!!

Had...13 Years living in Hawaii

Had...One Bankruptcy

Had...great friends

Had...a miscarriage

Had...at least 10 cars, 5 jobs and 3 careers

Had...two acquaintances who chose to commit suicide. (One in California, One in Hawaii)

Had...20+ Years in Sales:

Real Estate Sales…in both California / Hawaii

Medical Services Sales…in California

Financial / Banking Sales…in California

Selling myself and my "Weird Ideas"…to family, friends, business associates, and my Son Zachary, whose arrival in my life in 1986 has given me a WHY.

Had…a patent on a bag, that has long since expired

Had…the Choice to live a poor me existence, or "The World is a Great Place, full of fantastic people, be a part of it" existence!

Had…an able body, open mind and heart

Had…a love for the elderly

Had…to go to Hawaii

Had…to believe all people are created equal

Had…my beloved Grandfathers faith in people

Had…a need to be of assistance

Had…a Desire to Succeed

Had…a need to tell the World what I have been told and what I have seen

Had…no Choice, but to write this book

Had one Husband…"One Way to Go" & "Healer is a Loser"

ONE WAY TO GO

His eyes were deep blue with a sad and lonely stare

A" ten year marriage" just out like a flare

A new life to build a new world to share

A new love beside him to help him repair

His goals were set high, no doubt in his mind

He would achieve, great wealth and success of a kind

He was a mechanic, many years to his credit

His experience an asset if only he would let it

A business he started, auto repair was its aim

His skills as a mechanic brought moderate fame

A mechanic accomplished, a business man fair

The business flourished with cars everywhere

As the business got bigger, the more stress He created

His ability to cope, somehow, suddenly faded

Funny smoke and more beer, became his escape

As did building a race car while playing his tape

Deaf ear to his family, discarded his new Wife

He said to them all "Get out of my life!"

His friends all disbanded, this life thrown away

There is but one way to go and he started today

His eyes were deep blue with a sad lonely stare

A "three year marriage" just out like a flare

A new life to build a new world to share

A New Young love beside him to help him repair

THE HEALER

SHE ARRIVED SOON AFTER HE SUFFERED HIS HEARTBREAK

SHE PROVIDED THE SUPPORT THAT HEALING IT WOULD TAKE

SHE LOVED HIM, SHE COMFORTED HIM, SHE REBUILT HIS SELF ESTEEM

SHE CONVINCED HIM HE WAS HANDSOME, A MAN TO BE SEEN

HER LOVE SHE WOULD PROFESS TO HIM DAY BY DAY

NOT KNOWING THAT HEART BREAK WOULD SOON COME HER WAY

HIS CONFIDENCE RECOVERED, HIS MANHOOD RENEWED

HE LEFT HER ALONE FOR THE OTHERS TO BE PURSUED

A HEALER IS A LOSER DESTINED TO FAIL

WHEN INVESTING HER HEART IN A REBOUNDING MALE

THE PAIN AND THE ANGUISH OF TRYING TO SUPPORT

IS NOT WORTH THE EFFORT WHEN DEALING WITH THIS SORT

THE HEALING RELATIONSHIP IS A ONE SIDED GAME

WHERE THE HEALER GIVES ALL AND RECEIVES ONLY PAIN

AN END TO THIS SERVICE, NO MORE HEALING WILL SHE DO

HER HEART IS NOW BROKEN SHE HAS NO STRENGTH TO RENEW

YET TIME WILL PASS, HER HEART WILL MEND!

THE MAN! HER HEALER, HIS HAND, HE WILL EXTEND!

HAD...TO LEARN (1986), THAT I AM IN CONTROL OF HOW I RESPOND TO ALL THINGS, AND THAT LIFE IS TOO SHORT TO WALLOW IN THE MIRE!

HAD...to learn the power of forgiveness! And I did!

Had a Jaguar XJ6...Had a work ethic,...Had a Penthouse Close to Waikiki,...Had a desire for excellence

Had a house in Makakilo,...Had a wish to stay in Hawaii,...Had a love of Boogie boarding, Had terrible timing,...Had a love for sailing,...Had a Condo by the Ala Wai,... Had a Great Judge of Character,...

Had a Burning Desire to explain that suicide throw's GOD's Gift of Life back in his face. Anyone who encourages such a thing is going against the

23

teachings of God, Jesus, Moses, Mohammad, Allah, Buddha, Valhalla, Ganesh, and the Power of the Universe and is blind to the positive truth of life. Positive CHOICES! Create Positive SOLUTIONS!

HAD TO SAY…Following negative etiologies has and will lead Man toward becoming an endangered species. Positive teaching leads the way for Humans to connect with the same energy that makes trees grow, flowers bloom, and the fruit to appear on branches and vines.

HAD TO SAY…LIFE IS A GIFT. LIVE IT! CHOOSE TO GO TOWARD THE GOOD, NOT THE SHOULD. PEOPLE ARE GODS GIFT TO BE REMOVED FROM THIS EARTH BY WAY OF NATURAL CAUSES ONLY!

* ILLNESS, NATURAL DISASTERS, AND AT GODS WILL!

* NOT AT THE FREE WILL OF MAN!

HAD TO SAY…To intentionally take another Human Beings Life is not the will of any God known to man. Free will is the responsibility and personal choice of the individual made at his own risk. Humanity has denounced such acts as in-Humane, Evil/Retrograde behavior, and not worthy of mankind.

HAD TO SAY…JESUS MADE CHOICES, BUDDHA MADE CHOICES, MOHAMMED MADE CHOICES, AND MOSES MADE CHOICES.

ALL HUMANS HAD, HAVE AND WILL MAKE CHOICES.

WHAT ARE YOUR HADS?

1.

2.

3.

4.

5.

6.

7.

8.

9.

10.

11.

12.

13.

14.

15.

16.

17.

18.

19.

20.

21.

22.

23.

24.

Hads are Choices, Come and Gone!

COURAGE

IS THE PRICE THAT LIFE EXACTS,
FOR GRANTING PEACE!!
AMELIA EARHART (1898-1937)

CHAPTER 2

Have is a choice!

We all have a friend we consider a peer

Whose goal hasn't varied from year to year

Determination is strong in these people we've met

Their life is controlled by the Goals that they've set

We watch them grow while pursuing their end

Without a doubt they'll succeed, this dear friend

To know where we are going and not go astray

Is hard to accomplish for many today

The choice to Have is a goal we must set

In order to gauge how life's fulfillment is being met

Best wishes apply as we watch them progress

For fulfillment is LIFE is what they will possess

Life is today for we never know,

Will tomorrow come as a BLESSING, or come as a BLOW?

No guarantees, are allotted. Each day our thoughts create life. Our wisemen say.

Progress is made, when one discovers, "We are "Spiritual Beings, living a human life."

THINK! To Love all things great and good, is our Prime Directive.

HAVE, is what all people strive for in life. The pursuit of positive HAVE'S benefit's all of mankind. Connection with God, good health, love, wealth, the pursuit of happiness and Peace of Mind are all worthy HAVE'S. We have an innate desire to know what is beyond our universe. The pursuit of knowledge is also a Human must do. The pursuit of knowledge is endless.

On January 28, 1986, the world experienced a human disaster. The Shuttle Challenger was scheduled to "Soar to Glory" from its launching pad at Cape Canaveral, Florida. With seven of our nations brightest SOULS on board the world watched in anticipation. 74 seconds into the flight at 11:30 am, Florida time, the Challenger met with disaster. A tremendous explosion in mid-air brought a sudden end to its "Quest for Glory", causing all of our Astronauts on board to perish.

Our Nation and the world fell into a time of mourning. As I watched the memorial services on TV, I saw the sad, trembling family members and friends of the seven brave astronauts being supportive of each other. My thoughts were of the millions of people watching all over the world. Millions of Caring compassionate HUMAN BEINGS who felt personally touched by this great loss, all quietly whispering our own heartfelt messages of support.

Our President said, "The Sacrifice of our brave Challenger heroes has stirred the souls of a Nation", I believe the President would have been more accurate if he had said "The sacrifice of our brave Challenger Heroes has stirred the souls of the World."

For the first time in the History of Man, I saw in those seven special people as an culmination of what the family of man is made of. MEN, WOMEN, BLACK, WHITE, ASIAN, JEWISH, CHRISTIAN, BUDDHIST, SINGLE, MARRIED, MARRIED WITH CHILDREN, AND IN CHRISTA MCAULIFFE not only was she a mother, but she was the representative of children all over the world. As a Teacher she had their best interests at Heart.

On the day after the tragedy I kept feeling this nagging question. Why would GOD put together such a perfect example of all that is good about humanity only to destroy it for the entire World to see? WHY?? All my belief in a good and kind GOD was in conflict. WHY? WHY not let such groups succeed in a man-made endeavor to share and unite? No sooner had I asked the question then the answer appeared

I was living in beautiful Hawaii at the time. There the "ALOHA SPIRIT" (the Love of Man and Earth) lives and the sky is still clear enough for such an answer to be seen. On the day following the tragedy, I was driving on the Kalanianaole Highway along the back side of the extinct volcano, Diamond Head. At 7:00 a.m. Hawaiian time, I looked up and was awe struck by what I saw.

There on the horizon was an enormous, brightly colored orange full Moon. Flowing gently down the left rim of the Moon was a perfectly formed, Technicolor bright, RAINBOW. I'd never seen such a combination of RAINBOW and MOON in all my 37 years, thirteen of which were spent in Hawaii.

The MAGNIFICENCE of such a sight filled my heart with joy and my eyes with tears. The words to the song "SOME WHERE OVER THE RAINBOW" filled my head.

> Somewhere over the Rainbow way up high, there's a land that
> I heard of once in a lullaby. Somewhere over the Rainbow

skies are blue, and the dreams that you dare to dream really do come true.

Someday I'll wish upon a star and wake up where the clouds are far behind me.

Where troubles melt like lemon drops, away above the chimney tops.

That's where you'll find me.

Somewhere over the Rainbow Blue Birds fly, they fly over the rainbow why then of why can't I?

Even though this was a song from my childhood it connected me to my lost Heroes. The message seemed CLEAR. This could only be GOD telling the world that the SOULS of those seven brave people are safe and with HIM. They are now one with the Universe.

If the flight had succeeded, as planned, they would have been Americans who achieved a brief taste of glory. In their deaths, they are HUMANS who became united in spirit and purpose. They have all become one with the Universe and are united with GOD to help us still here on Earth, to find the same love and understanding for one another that they had to find before they could have ventured beyond the Earth's plane.

With the events in Eastern Europe, Glasnost in Russia, and the destroying of the Berlin Wall only four years after CHALLENGER, I believe I must have been only one of the millions of Humans who got the message.

CHRISTIANS: Might say "The Lord Works in Mysterious Ways"

NEW AGE PEOPLE: Might say "Their positive energy will help raise the EARTH'S Vibration toward love and understanding of one another bringing true Peace."

PEOPLE WHO BELIEVE IN REINCARNATION: Might say "Individually their souls were many, many ages old and they evolved to the point that they have joined the Universal Power. GOD, MOHAMMED, JESUS, BUDDHA, MOSES, ALLAH, VALHALLA, Which ever you chose to call this Universal Power...

THE UN-INTERESTED! TOO BUSY, BELIEVERS IN NOTHING!: Might say "Seven People Died"

DICTATORS! DESPOTS!, AND REBEL LEADERS!: Would say "What shuttle? What mission to fly into space??" They have not been interested in joining the rest of the World. Their only interest has been in their own pursuit of power and control of the people of their country or region. As we open our minds, and our hearts, such leaders as these will disappear.

I for one believe, "They Slipped the Surly Bonds of Earth to Touch the Face of God" for the sake of Mankind.

Thank You…Dick Scobee

Thank You…Judy Resnik/Shalom

Thank You…Michael Smith

Thank You…Ellision Onizuka (Mahalo & Aloha)

Thank You…Ronald McNair

Thank You…Greg Jarvis

Thank You…Christa McAuliffe (in the name of my son Zachary, born 1986)

Christa had a desire to teach children to be all they could be and not let false or imaginary limitations get in their way. My son's future is so open, so bright and full of opportunities thanks to them all.

Through our Voyager Space Probes we have reached the outer limits of our solar system as we know it. We are now probing far into the unknown Space. Change is upon us. "Let go and let GOD," knowing all is well is our Universe. "There is nothing to fear, except fear itself." Franklin Roosevelt

12 years after the first Shuttle disaster, on September 11, 2001 the growth, peace, and balance of our world changed again. I was forced to re-think my original vision of the family of man. I learned that I'd been mistaken in 1986. Sadly it took this tragedy and the death of thousands of innocent people by way of natural disasters for me to see my mistake.

A whole segment of people were not represented by the crew of the Shuttle Challenger. The people of the Middle East at that point had not been an active participant in the family of mans endeavor to venture beyond our Earth Plane. Today they are still reluctant to join in or allow people of the West to become part of their Universe.

We have been yanked back from our endeavor to reach the heights and have been forced to address our relationships with our fellow human beings in the Middle Eastern part of our World.

We need to connect with the individuals who are not aware that they are connected to the rest of our shared universe. We need to find their adult leaders. The leaders who truly have their best interest at heart. They need to know we are all together on this planet we call Earth. We all need the same air, the same water, and the same sun. Once a human becomes aware of their relationship and true connection to every other human on earth it becomes harder to hurt a fellow human being.

To the detriment of the rest of the World an angry hate filled man emerged from the Middle East. This disgruntled Human Being named Osama Bin Laden had a privileged life. He was a son of a wealthy contractor with ties to the Saudi Royal Family. Somewhere along the way he developed hatred, anger, jealousy and a feeling of irrelevancy. He became disconnected. He needed to show the world that he was here on earth and needed to draw attention to himself. It appears to me that like Hitler, Osama Bin Laden's anger and frustration was nurtured by his overall hatred toward his father or lack of a caring, nurturing father.

His acts of Terrorism, such as the attack on the World by way of the destruction of the World Trade Center and all such attacks since, are the action of an angry, spoiled child in a an adult body who is not mature enough to get the attention of adults in power. As would a child, he lashed out in a destructive negative way, harming the world as a whole. Now the only attention he can expect to receive in return, from responsible adults, is negative. Like a child he cared not for anyone but himself, with no thought of consequences for his actions. He had a spoiled child's temper tantrum; "To hell with the rest of the World" was his attitude and his choice.

We can forgive and correct a child, but once that damage is in the mind and the body of a grown adult, as in the case of many such individuals as Osama bin Laden, they must blame everyone but themselves for their unhappiness and anger. Hitler had the Jews to blame, Stalin had anyone who didn't agree with him, Saddam Hussein had the Kurds and the Shiites, and now bin Laden has Western men, women, children or anyone else including Muslims who disagree with his warped interpretation of the Quran.

With his skewed view of the Quran and the Western world, his little boy like anger, and all the time and financial resources to feed his anger, it manifested. As a grown man he became lethal with a childlike solution to his problem.

Osama bin Laden's goal and method to seek and destroy is so far against the teachings of GOD / Allah that his only purpose is to destroy what GOD has created. He can never prevail nor will any such individual with Evil/Retrograde thinking.

JOURNAL: SEPTEMBER 11, 2001

Today at about 8:45 AM Eastern Standard Time the United States of America was attacked by Radical Muslim Fanatic's under the control of Osama Bin Laden who resides in Afghanistan.

The attack consisted of the commandeering of 4 US Passenger Flight Aircraft:

> The First plane, At 7:59 am EDT American flight 11 from Boston to Los Angeles with 81 passengers, and 11 crew on board, was flown as a guided missile into the North Tower of the International Trade Center. All onboard perished.

> The Second plane, at 8:14 am, United Flight 175, from Boston to Los Angeles, 56 passengers 9 crew, hits the South Tower. All onboard perished.

35

The Third plane: At 8:01 United Airlines Flight 93, Newark to San Francisco, 38 passengers 7 crew, was diverted from its intended target, The Capital Building" and forced to crash as its Brave passengers attempted to retake the plane. Some passengers had been informed by family and friends by way of cell phones, of the intentions of the Highjackers. The plane crashes at Stoney Creek, Pa. All on board perished.

The forth plane was flown into the Pentagon; all on board perished.

Reports have started coming in. 5,000 people are missing and presumed dead in the Twin Towers, 3,000 are injured. (Death toll estimated at 3,000, with 400,000 counseled since then)

This Tragedy could be described as a combination of the following world renowned Movies:

Towering Inferno
Armageddon
Final Impact
Air Force One
Diehard 1, 2 & 3 with very bad endings.

The fire, the smoke, the brave citizens on the flight in Pensylvania was horrific. The total destruction of planes, buildings, and innocent lives at the hands of fanatic American Haters is a man made catastrophe. Men utilized their Free Will from God and Chose EVIL/Retrograde behavior.

President GW Bush has called for war with Bin Laden and his Terrorist Cells throughout the World in approximately 10 Countries. Reports are saying PEOPLE from 50 Nations were killed in the Twin Towers.

Here I am feeling sorry for myself because I am temporarily out of a job. How silly. We Will Survive, We will prevail, and we will endure. "GOD BLESSES AMERICA".

Tonight 9/19/2001, The President addressed the Congress and the Nation. We are going after Terrorists worldwide. Troops are deployed. May GOD have mercy on all of his Children, good, bad, and innocent.

The Afghanistan Mullahs are saying, "If we attack Afghanistan we will have a Jihad, or Holy War." There is nothing holy about War.

The Middle Easterners haven't become aware nor do they understand all that God has given us in America. We have been blessed and believe in the equal rights of man. We have been given;

The ability to live free with other religions.

The ability to inter-communicate in an adult responsible manner.

The unity which comes from mutual respect and malice toward none.

The desire for Peace and the gift of cooperation.

Our access to endless forms of Communication and desire to use them.

We need to reach out to the Middle East, instead of waiting for them to attack us. Hate is always defeated by Love. Time Will Tell. I've always believed in "With MALICE TOWARD NONE."

9/21/2001 Watching and listening to a tribute to Hero's on TV. There are many celebrities singing and telling stories of inspiration and Love.

My Tribute…Close your Eyes

The Towers Sustain…the Towers Remain,

The Souls of many…No more pain.

The Love they sent…while unknown their Fate

Invisible the Towers…Let's Make no mistake

The strength… the Love…that was real

The Towers… they remain…Hidden from Our View

Innocent Souls…Pray with one Breath

Proclaimed in death…but the Towers Remain

Tall and Strong…Our loved ones there…Remain! The Towers Sustain!

The tears have been endless for 10 days. Reports are constantly changing, now they say 80 countries had citizens killed in the Towers? The Stock Market is down; Airlines laying off, Marines sent to War, The Tribute to Hero's and lost loved ones is continuous…

9/24/2001 "The Taliban ready for Holy War!"

9/25/2001 for two weeks now I have been listening to stories of Coincidence, fate & faith. All along I've been trying to find the collective meaning. Catastrophes seem to always have a collective message. **The theme** that is constant seems to be **Father** and **Son.**

The first story I heard was the story of Cantor Fitzgerald (a Bond Company) located in the First Tower. The company lost 700 employees, including one of the Partners. Two brothers were the partner owners. One perished with his staff. The other brother / CEO of the company survived because he was doing what a **Good Father** needs to do. He was late to work that day because he was escorting his young **son** to his first day of preschool. Approximately 1,500 children were left without a **father or possibly a mother.**

Another story was of a **Father** whose 12-year-old son was on the flight that struck the Pentagon. The boy won a contest at school and had been awarded a trip as an Honor. Ironically, the **father** had taken the day off from work to take his son to the airport or he would have been sitting at his desk in the Pentagon where the plane carrying his **Son** struck. He's son, the rest of the planes passengers and 30 of his fellow employees perished that day.

There were two Airline flight attendants that had been life-long friends. One attendant was on the plane that struck the First Tower; the other attendant, along with her 8-year-old daughter was on the other plane striking the Second Tower. The Brother and Husband of these attendants were just leaving the First Tower as the planes struck. Fortunately, they both survived.

A **father** and **son** were both New York City Firemen and were both lost when the Towers Collapsed.

A young woman was frantic when she heard about the tragedy. Her **father** was on one of the ill-fated flights. She had just had a big argument with him that morning before he left. She was now left with a should "and Shoulds Don't Count!"

Former President George H Bush, during a memorial Service consoled his son, George W. Bush our current President.

A beloved Monsignor/Chaplain for the Fire Department also perished.

At least two of the brave citizens of the Pennsylvania United Airlines Flight 93 were brand **new fathers** who were killed along with all onboard after they tried to subdue the highjackers and avoid crashing into the Capital Building. They were able to contact their spouses on the ground to let them know they loved them and to be strong for their Children.

Then there are the Terrorists themselves who came from an environment where gentle love is unheard of. They were taught as boys to fight and hate at a very early age. The balance of love and nurturing is stifled by a doctrine that suppresses women disallowing them to participate in their society. They were raised in an environment where the forsaking of one's wife, mother, and daughter is considered manly. I find it hard to believe that any mother, if given the option, would choose to allow their sons to kill, fight or commit suicide.

The modern world has long since refused to create the images of Women wailing over dead **sons**, husbands, brothers, and uncles, **fathers** and **grandfathers** on the battlefield.

Two men, two cultures, fight over an issue. After the battle has ended the same two men are still standing, fighting over the same issue while the rest of their armies and humanity are casualties and their feet. This type of reaction to a problem has yet to provide a positive result for humanity!

The solution to such a conflict lie with finding and resolving the issue between the entities involved before the World, as a whole, became a casualty.

A Childhood tale was made into a movie shown worldwide. "Hook" the story of Peter Pan, all grown up. In a scene, the villainous Captain Hook and his Pirates are trying to corrupt the adult Peter's young children. Hook convinces the little boy that his **father** didn't care for him because he neglected him for work and other adults. The little girl tries to remind her brother of the gentle and caring love of his mother. The little girl sings a song expressing their mother's love. She tells Captain Hook and all the Pirates that they are very bad men and they need their mommy! While hearing the girl sing the pirates and Captain Hook become teary eyed thinking of their mothers. When the gentle voice of a little girl can be heard and acknowledged as relevant, by the pirates of the world, maybe we will have a chance at peace.

The **Balance** of Mothers Love and **Fathers Love** is what creates a healthy society. Until the hate emanating from the souls of the terrorists can be softened by love for their fellow man the World must brace itself for the repercussions from lessons in tough love that the rest of the World must teach Osama Bin Laden and his followers.

Love will always conquer Evil/Retrograde thinking

Free the Women of the Middle East. Offer them a true way to save their men and sons

From disaster!

The World needs to learn and teach Fatherly love for all human beings by all

Other Human beings

Love is what our collective **Father/GOD** offers…Never hate or violence.

GOD made it simple we, the Human occupants of our planet, make it difficult.

In history there is an example of a man who was physically small in stature, but emotionally mature enough to come up with the most effective way to accomplish what he wanted for himself and his fellow countrymen. Mahatma Gandhi's method of non-violence accomplished his goal for his people by showing them how to take responsibility for the way they treat themselves and others.

He brought a powerful Nation to its knees, with his rejection of violence and won the support of the people of the World. He took responsibility for his desire for change. With courage and righteousness he took the pain and ridicule upon himself and his followers. He spoke against violence and killing as a solution to anything. This man was a man worth listening too and following. The brave live and endure until they accomplish what they want in regard to change. Death by murder or suicide is a waste of human life which is not ours to take. God, Jesus, Buddha, Mohammad, whatever you wish to call our God has created a world where everyone has an opportunity to live free, productive, and caring lives.

Gandhi was a True Adult, a Leader, and a man of God. His method captured the minds and hearts of his enemy and brought the result he desired. He was a positive leader not a follower of darkness. Martin Luther King followed Gandhi's example and made the world better for his people by following the positive teachings of GOD. Violence has never created a positive and lasting result. Shoulds don't count toward anything lasting and good.

Today we / the World have two choices as to how we wish to perceive success:

#1 The choice we had before 9-11

To laugh often and much

To win the respect of intelligent people and the affection of children

To earn the appreciation of honest critics and endure the betrayal of fake

Friends

To appreciate beauty

To find the best in others, whether by a healthy child, a garden patch, or

Redeemed social condition.

To know even one life has breathed easier because you have lived.

This is to have succeeded!...**Ralph Waldo Emerson**

#2 The Choice created by Osama Bin Laden 9/11

To prey often and much on the innocent

To create fear in intelligent people and the total oppression of women and Children

To earn the appreciation of fellow terrorists and murderers

To injure and betray all free people of the World

To destroy all beauty

To find the worst in all people

To leave the World a bitter place, whether by a hate filled child, minefield, or

A destroyed Social Condition.

To know even 5 lives have ended because you have died

This is to have succeeded, Osama Bin Laden's Way

Osama's choice brings man away from the light and into darkness. This negative path obscures our vision of a good and healthy life. There is no win here only turmoil, misery, and eternal darkness.

GOD, (JESUS, MOHAMMAD, BUDDHA, MOSES, VALHALLA, GANESHA, OR THE POWER OF THE UNIVERSE), whatever you choose to call such power would not want this for his children!!

Hate is the mantra for Osama's type of success. This is the true nature of something "Other than GOD, Something that promotes negative hurtful and harmful living not worthy of Man.

Hitler used his warped view of the teachings of the Bible to validate his Evil/Retrograde behavior. Osama Bin Laden uses his warped view of the teachings of the Koran to validate his Evil/Retrograde behavior. Stalin oppressed the teaching of all religion to promote his plan.

I used to wonder what Osama's Bin Laden's had's and have's were. Today, we know he was consumed and drowning in his own Should. (2001-2012)

Followers of hate / retrograde thinking are takers who are disconnected from what is good on our planet. Evolving from aggression is coming into the light and discovering we are spiritual beings worthy of one others love and respect. Living with grace and compassion is courageous.

One evening an old Cherokee told his grandson about a battle that goes on inside people...

He said, "My son, there is battle between the two "wolves" that are inside us all.

One is Evil- it is anger, envy, jealousy, sorrow, regret, greed, arrogance, self-pity, guilt, resentment, inferiority, lies, false pride, superiority, and ego.

The other is Good- it is joy, peace, love, hope, serenity, humility, kindness, benevolence, empathy, generosity, truth, compassion, and faith."The grandson thought about it for a minute and then asked his grandfather: "Which wolf wins?

The old Cherokee simply replied, "The one you feed.

CHILDREN LEARN WHAT THEY LIVE

IF A CHILD LIVES WITH CRITICISM,

HE LEARNS TO CONDEMN.

IF A CHILD LIVES WITH HOSTILITY,

HE LEARNS TO FIGHT.

IF A CHILD LIVES WITH RIDICULE,

HE LEARNS TO BE SHY.

IF A CHILD LIVES WITH TOLERANCE,

HE LEARNS TO BE PATIENT.

IF A CHILD LIVES WITH ENCOURAGEMENT,

HE LEARNS CONFIDENCE.

D. C. Williams

IF A CHILD LIVES WITH PRAISE,

HE LEARNS TO APPRECIATE.

IF A CHILD LIVES WITH FAIRNESS,

HE LEARNS JUSTICE.

IF A CHILD LIVES WITH SECURITY,

HE LEARNS TO HAVE FAITH.

IF A CHILD LIVES WITH APPROVAL,

HE LEARNS TO LIKE HIMSELF.

IF A CHILD LIVES WITH ACCEPTANCE AND FRIENDSHIP,

HE LEARNS TO FIND LOVE IN THE WORLD.

Dorothy Lau Nolte

RISK 2005

TO WEAR SOMETHING OTHER THAN BLACK

TO INTERACT WITH SOMEONE NOT OF YOUR RELIGION

TO BE OPEN TO BEAUTY, CHANGE, AND LIFE

TO BELIEVE YOU ARE A PART OF THE UNIVERSE, A BROTHER OR SISTER to YOUR FELLOW HUMAN BEINGS.

TO BELIEVE MOST PEOPLE ARE GOOD AND CARING. JUST A FEW ARE EVIL.

TO BELIEVE IT IS RIGHT THAT OTHER RELIGIONS EXIST

TO SHOW YOUR FACE AND EXPRESS YOUR FEELINGS

TO SAY NO TO SACRIFICING YOUR LIFE AND THAT OF A LOVED ONE TO SUICIDE AND MURDER

TO SOLVE A PROBLEM WITHOUT VIOLENCE

TO SAY NO TO HATE AND VIOLENCE

TO UNITE IN PEACE, FOR PEACE, AS A BELIEVER IN PEACE

TO OPPOSE HATE AND MURDER FOR ANY REASON

TO BELIEVE YOUR CHILDREN DESERVE A FULL LIFE, FULL OF LOVE AND LAUGHTER, AS DO OTHER CHILDREN.

TO BELIEVE YOUR CHILDREN HAVE A FUTURE WORTH LIVING

TO KNOW A SHOULD FREE LIFE IS PURE **RISK,** "WITH MALICE TOWARD NONE." AND BEST WISHES TOWARD ALL

TO KNOW LIVING A LIFE OF PEACE AND LOVE IS WORTHY AND NECESSARY FOR THE CHILDREN

TO ACKNOWLEDGE THE HAD AND TERMINATE THE SHOULD

TO HAVE PEACE OF MIND!!

Dcw1985

D. C. Williams

MY HAVE'S:

Have a Life

Have a Son, who is healthy, wealthy, wise, and happy

Have my brother, sister and many nieces, nephews, grandnieces and grandnephews.

Have 10 Aunts and Uncles

Have 20 plus Cousins

Have a 1995 car paid in full

Have a belief that the good people outnumber the bad

Have many friends and colleagues

Have my health

Have bills and taxes to pay

Have dreams of creating a community for elderly

Have dreams of a should free world

Have a Real Estate Career

Have a love of life

Have hope for a peaceful world for my Son and his children

Have assets and liabilities

Have a turquoise ring my grandmother left me

Have a pearl necklace given to me by a wonderful person named Grace

Have a patent on a bag that has long since expired

Have many reasons for living

Have a plan for the next 10 years

Have an adopted step sister whose doctors couldn't make a choice to do surgery or not. They should on each other and she became disabled. "Shoulds" doesn't count!!

Have a few quotes and sayings that I live by;

"With malice toward none" Abe Lincoln

"I am Healthy, Wealthy, Wise and Happy"

"Do unto others as you would have others do unto you"

"Life, Liberty, and the pursuit of happiness"

"Only the weak revert to violence, the strong negotiate and everyone wins"

"This is the beginning of a new day. GOD has given me this day to use as I will. I can waste it or use it for Good, but what I do today is important, because I am exchanging a Day of My Life for it. I want it to be Gain and Not Loss: Good and Not Evil: Success and Not Failure: in order that I shall not regret the price that I paid for it." Dr. Heartstill Wilson

Have good Memories that I Cherish

Have a need to validate and be validated. We are all Relevant!

Have a Life to Live, Places to go, People to see

Have Faith in Men who are not intimidated by strong supportive Women

Have a Brother who loves to Fish

Have a Sister who loves Her Children

Have been blessed with 4 Adopted Cousins and Numerous Step Relatives

Have appreciation for all who invested their time in My Life

Have a Vision of Reality not easily accepted by others

Have no need to see negative in others in order to be positive with myself

Have a very Large Extended Family with every aspect of life represented

Have been looking for Balance in My Life for the last 30 years

Have appreciation for an Old Cliché such as "The Cup is Half Full, Not Half Empty"

Have many Questions

Have endless Solutions

Have a multitude of options

Have lessons learned and lessons yet to be re-learned

Have my Eyes Open, looking for new answers

Have every reason in the World to believe every human being wants to LAUGH!

Have a great respect for those who can create a valid reason to Laugh

Have no desire to ever hold a grudge for any reason

Have given up feeling guilty, less than, better than, and afraid of being a victim

Have become an adult, the "Buck Stops Here"

Have decided that Peter Pan's Wendy grew up and so can I

Have given up believing I have to make someone else wrong in order to be right

Have decided to enjoy my Have's and acquire more, as long as I can

WHAT ARE YOUR HAVES?

1.

2.

3.

4.

5.

6.

7.

8.

9.

10.

11.

12.

13.

14.

15.

Have/Had are the Brick and Mortar of
Life! Have is Life, Here and Now!

RESPONSIBILITY: "ABLE TO RESPOND"
FALSE DEFINITION: "BLAME, SHAME, GUILT"

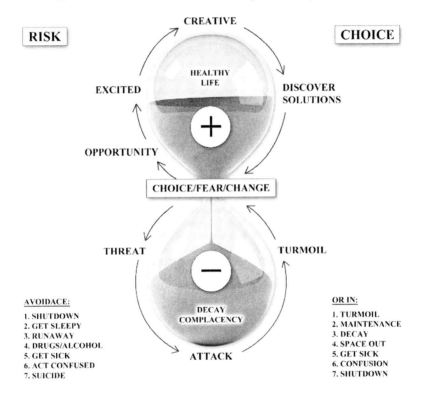

CHAPTER 3

SHOULD is a choice!

Should doesn't count! Once Should appears it is too late, the choice to do or not to do has already been made. The damage and the consequences have already been felt.

Example: We choose our actions without regard to consequences to ourselves and others.

We should take the baby out of the car when we exit

When, "We took the baby out of the car when we exited!" is the only course.

We should lock the gun in the cabinet away from the children.

When, "We locked the gun in the cabinet!" is the only course of action.

True responsible adults choose the difficult path of action if it will address the problem, and protect from harm all the living, especially the children.

Should doesn't count. Only did counts. "LIFE IS TOO SHORT FOR SHOULD"

WHILE IN HONOLULU, I assisted a man who told me his story of "Should's don't count." This man was paralyzed on one side from a stroke, blind in one eye, and he shuffled around slowly using a special crutch tucked under his right shoulder. He and his brother were joint owners in a large chain of well known restaurants throughout Hawaii and Florida, USA

This is his story as I remember him telling it to me:

I had a beautiful home on the windward side of Kaneohe Bay, on the Island of Oahu, where I lived with my wonderful wife and my 8 year old Son. I worked very hard to maintain my chain of restaurants and was away from home for days at a time. When I did come home my Son would ask me if I would take him fishing in the bay. I told my Son sorry I can't this time, but I will when I get back again.

When I returned after a 5 day business trip my Son was there to greet me. He was very happy and hugged me so tight as if he never wanted to let me go. I said "Ok, Son! We'll go fishing tomorrow, OK!" My Son hugged me again and said with a big grin, "I'll be ready in the morning." The next day my Son greeted me at breakfast, but before he could say I'm ready to go, the phone rang, it was my buddies. They were all going to play golf at the Waialae Country

Club and wanted me to join them. I said "sure, I'll meet you there in about an hour." My son said, "Dad you promised you'd take me fishing." I said back to him, "Son, I haven't seen these guys in a long time. I promise I'll take you fishing tomorrow, I promise, OK!" I was happy to be going golfing. I told my Son Bye. I'll see you when I get back. I left and didn't even give him a hug goodbye.

While I was on the 18th hole, I received a phone call from my frantic, sobbing wife. She said, "Our Son is missing. He was so hurt about not going fishing with you that he decided to go boogie boarding in the bay, by himself. "They found his ripped and bloody boogie board and believe a shark got him." A few days later they found evidence that our worst fears were true. My beautiful 8 year old Son had been all alone in the bay and was killed by a shark.

He sobbed, my son is gone, my wife is gone, my house on Kaneohe Bay is gone, and I turned the business over to my brother who pays me a small salary every month. I HAD everything I wanted!

The pain this man's choice created was apparent in his trembling body and his cracked voice. The tears rolling down his cheeks appeared to be burning trails in his tormented face. Physical Therapy was not enough to ease the pain in this man's soul. I never saw him again and don't know if he ever found peace in his life.

His second choice to keep the guilt and not channel it toward a positive cause had created his present state. He is shoulding on himself daily. Punishing himself daily. Instead of realizing that Should's don't count. Instead of honoring his son's short life it is all about himself. His guilt is greater than the eight years of his son's life. Instead of honoring the memory, the essence and the joy his son brought him during his short life time, he is focused on himself. What he didn't do! What he lost! What he didn't give! What he didn't get!

What if his pain, guilt, anger and remorse had been transmuted into positive action? Such as the creation of a memorial or a donation to a library, or school for fatherless boys in the name of his son. The man never mentioned his son by name. A positive and a negative cannot occupy the same space. He needed to revere his son in a way which could help him heal.

The negative cycle this type of choice creates is apparent. The suffering in the Middle East today is similar kind of cycle. The pain, anguish, guilt, anger and remorse of past deeds have been perpetuated by generation after generation of negative action. It is time to create positive deeds in order to overcome the negative HADS of the World.

Mahatma Gandhi discovered the key of positive action and used it. He would not participate in a negative or violent manner. He broke the cycle of negative and hateful action which had enslaved not only his country but had also enslaved the country of the people who were in power. Victory by positive action is more productive, effective and self-perpetuating in the long run.

Victory by negative action is never a victory. It breeds constant conflict and perpetuates the cycle of guilt, pain, anger, remorse and revenge. Why would anyone choose to surround themselves with negative energy that is dark and heavy, when positive energy and action is illuminating and light as a feather. A clear Soul and Spirit allows one to know they can soar above any and all adversity placed at their feet.

Jesus said, "Turn the other cheek." Mahatma Gandhi, a Hindu, did just that and created positive perpetuating results. Then evil (retrograde followers) responded with negative action and the cycle starts again. LET US CHOOSE POSITIVE ACTION FOR POSITIVE RESULTS. GOD GAVE US FREE WILL! KILLING WAS NEVER PART OF THE EQUATION.

When I was eight years old;

There were two 8 year old neighborhood boys who were inseparable. Their friendship was unusual especially for the mid 1960's. One boy was blond, a true toe head. The other boy was in those days, Negro (civil rights were just on the horizon). They were the nicest boys you would ever want to meet. They smiled a lot and always seemed to be having fun. Where one was, there was the other. They couldn't have been more like brothers without truly being brothers. They didn't need a protest to know they were equal.

One day they were playing alone at one of their homes. Being home alone wasn't unusual, majority of parents worked. They came across a shotgun hidden in the closet. They played hunter and deer all afternoon without pulling the trigger. The boys new the rules and were very careful.

At 5pm it was time for one of them to go home. Abruptly, one of the boys shouted "BYE!" and ran out the kitchen door kiddingly, teasingly he yelled back, "You can't shoot me now! HA! Ha!" The boy with the rifle, still laughing, turned quickly to say goodbye TO HIS FRIEND. The screen door SLAMMED! And startled him, he jerked and accidentally squeezed the trigger, throwing him back to the floor. Buckshot went through the kitchen door, killing his best friend instantly. When the neighbors found the boys, one boy was lying on the grass bleeding profusely. The other boy was sobbing while kneeling next to his friend begging him to please wake up. The gun was on the kitchen floor where it landed when he ran to his friend's side.

The pain and anguish, that not locking up the gun in a secure place, caused will never go away. There are two young lives devastated. Their families are forever tainted. Adults don't let the innocent suffer needlessly.

These two boys were way beyond their time when it came to love and understanding of your fellow man, but too young to truly understand the power of a loaded weapon

Wisdom and compassion taught to our young would be far more valuable in the aggregate then learning to fire or not fire a gun.

The innocent must be protected, especially by the adults who love them

From 1999-2002 there were numerous incidents where an infant or young child had been left in a car seat, firmly strapped in a car to protect them. The windows rolled up, the temperature outside greater than 100 degrees. The parent or caregiver walked away and forgot the child in the car?

I once found a child locked in a car parked in the grocery store parking lot. It was 110 degrees outside, the windows were rolled up, and he had a jacket on. I rushed into the store and told the manager to page for the parent and call the police.

A lady came running down the aisle smiling and giggling. She was waving her arms saying, "It's me. But that isn't even my child, I'm just baby-sitting." This was the adult entrusted with the life and safety of someone's child?? Luckily the little boy was ok.

Many times the children are found or remembered too late. Once the should appears it is too late. The damage and the consciences have already been felt. The devastating results are irreversible.

Which adult let that child down the most? The baby-sitter or the parent who chose her?

Such acts as these can be avoided by removing distractions with things that have no value and attaching a much greater value to our children and all living beings.

SHOULDS DON'T COUNT!!!

In the not so distant past, about 5 months before September 11, 2001 a local woman from Corona, California got news that her husband had been one of a number of American tourists kidnapped from an exclusive Resort in the Philippines. These rebels were said to be one of the most brutal in all of the Philippines and had executed one of their prisoners.

Within days it was confirmed that her husband was the man who was viciously murdered by his captors. This was the first broadly acknowledged execution of that sort and the beginning of many such terrorist executions. The irony of this story is that her husband was supposed to be on a fishing trip with his buddies, but decided to take his girlfriend on a romantic getaway instead. His wife and children were devastated to hear the news. It is obvious that her husband regretted his choice.

D. C. Williams

SHOULD'S DON'T COUNT!!!

"Thou shalt not kill"

"Thou shalt not lie"

"Thou shalt not covet thy neighbor's wife"

WE MUST REMEMBER WE ARE RESPONSIBLE FOR THE CHOICES WE MAKE UNDER THE PREMISE OF FREE WILL.

THE EVIL DOERS (RETROACTIVE THINKERS), TOOK THIS MAN'S LIFE UTILIZING THEIR FREE WILL. EVIL DOERS TAKE, THEY NEVER GIVE. THIS WAS OBVIOUSLY A SENSELESS ACT COMMITTED AT THE WILL OF SOMETHING OTHER THAN GOD. TRYING TO ACCOMPLISH ANYTHING THROUGH EVIL DEEDS WILL NEVER CREATE A POSITIVE RESULT.

WHO DO YOU KNOW IS STUCK IN THE MIRE OF THEIR PAINFUL STORY?

1.

2.

3.

4.

5.

6.

7.

8.

LIFE IS TOO SHORT TO WALLOW IN THE MIRE!

THE LAST WISH:

In 1995 I made a choice which has been a catalyst to my need for clarity of what is important in life. I used to pride myself on my ability to empathize with people. I thought that 17 years of providing Physical Therapy for the physically impaired had given me that clarity. This incident proved to me that I was wrong in my assumption.

I befriended a lovely couple, Phil and Grace Hunter, both in their early 80's. They were well educated, well traveled, and sharp as a tack. Grace mentioned she needed help with Phil who had become weakened in the last few months. They had no children and were dependent on one another for support. A couple of days a week I would help Grace get Phil to bed at night and up in the morning.

One day, while getting Phil up, I noticed a lump in the middle of his chest. I was almost positive it was an aortic aneurysm. I helped Grace take Phil to the doctor. The doctor explained to the Hunters that Phil had an aneurysm that needed to be repaired but Phil's chance of surviving the surgery was unlikely. Phil decided to live with the aneurysm as long as it would allow.

About a month later, at 1 pm in the afternoon, I received a call from Grace. She said, "Phil passed away this afternoon. Would you come and stay with me while they come to take Phil away? I said, "of course, I will be right there." We sat and held hands while the mortuary representatives took Phil away. Grace told me about the many beautiful years she and Phil had spent together living in Aruba and traveling throughout Europe.

Grace said, "I want to die in my bed like Phil, could you help me with that? I said, "Grace, I am not a family member, I'm not sure I can promise you and make sure that happens, but I will do my best when the time comes."

I just started a new position as a traveling Representative for a medical group which took me away for days at a time. Upon my return from a trip I learned Grace had a stroke and was taken to a local Hospital. I hurried to the hospital. The stroke paralyzed Grace on the right side taking away her ability to speak.

She had been such a beautiful communicator. With a degree in History/Art from the University of California, Berkeley, she was eloquent in her conversation. The loss of speech was the most devastating of all. Grace never wanted to be placed in an infirmary and was unable to protest. Without a designated representative she was at the mercy of the system.

As a non-relative I was very limited and only allowed to visit because I convinced the staff that I was a cousin. One day Grace was transferred to a care home. When I visited she reached up to me and pointed to her wheelchair as if to go home. My fear of the consequences, which I would have, for taking her out of the hospital stopped me from taking her home to her bed right then. I told myself, I would call her real cousin that night when I left the home.

At 2am that morning Grace Darling Hunter died. I was too late to give her the last wish of dying at home in her bed.

I will always regret my weakness. I promised myself if ever I am placed in a similar situation I will opt to accept the consequences and make sure that I honor the last wished of a dying friend.

Forgive me Grace, you deserved better than you got and I deserve to follow through with what I know is right. SHOULD'S DON'T COUNT!

In this day and age, I recommend anyone concerned with how they will spend their last days of life make a video/documented Will. If there is ever a question of how you wish and are to be treated, a video will address it. Make the video while you are healthy and clear!

D. C. Williams

Grace had more than enough funds in her estate to insure she was taken care of at home. Her wish was to pass with the dignity she deserved. The Hunters didn't have a child or a designated friend or organization legally appointed to follow through with her wishes.

A Bank or other organization assigned to handle a person's trust can also be required per last will and testament/video will, etc., to provide the needed funds to pay a loving family member or medical personnel to care for an individual in their home or desired location until they pass.

"SHOW SOME RESPECT FOR A GREAT GENERATION"

Tom Brokaw, the Greatest Generation

There is a special generation of people who went through the CRASH OF 1929, the GREAT DEPRESSION OF 1932, funded WORLD WAR II starting in 1941, sent it's kid brothers to KOREA, sent it's sons to VIETNAM, and sent it's grandchildren to the PERSIAN GULF WAR.

They paid for the MARSHALL PLAN and the BERLIN AIRLIFT, SENT men to the MOON, explored deep space and won the COLD WAR through heavy taxes.

Go to Rest Homes and Senior Citizen Centers. Look even in your own family and you will find these people who did more than any Generation in History.

They might walk a little bent over, because they carried a heavy load. You don't have to put up monuments to them; they did that already by leaving a greater America.

We are losing these treasures, more every day. Soon they will all be gone.

Tomorrow is not guaranteed, preparing may bring peace of mind?

On this narrow Planet, We have only the choice between two unknown worlds.

Colette (1873-1954)

CHAPTER 4

Shouldless

In the overall scheme of Life very few things have true social, financial, physical, and emotional value. One thing that would provide great value to the world as a whole is the elimination of the SHOULD MENTALITY altogether.

SHOULD/MANANA':

Is the root of all evil (retrograde thinking)!

The foundation of procrastination

The perpetuation of the turmoil throughout the world

The biggest obstacle to humanity acquiring Clarity for what is truly important in life

We need to get control of our FREE WILL!

When we use our FREE WILL and choose greed, World Markets suffer!

When we use our FREE WILL and do the right thing we eliminate the should and build equity in life.

WILL: The desire and power to control by mental force. To make positive or negative things happen. To have the determination to eliminate the should and avoid a retrograde existence...

There is a car bumper sticker that reads:

"THE WINNER DIES WITH THE MOST TOYS!"

I believe:

"THE WINNER DIES WITHOUT A SHOULD ON THEIR LAST BREATH."

LAST BREATH

I LAY HERE IN SILENCE, UNABLE TO SPEAK

MY FATE UNKNOWN FROM WEEK TO WEEK

MY BODY A PRISON, I'M UNABLE TO FLEE

ALL THAT IS AROUND ME I AM UNABLE TO SEE

THE SOUNDS I HEAR ARE VAGUE AND UNCLEAR

THE LIFE I CLING TO, I CLING TO IN FEAR

I HESITATE TO LEAVE THIS EARTH BOUND SHELL

FOR THE LOVED ONES AROUND ME
SURROUND ME SO WELL

WARMTH AND BRIGHT LIGHT DESCEND LIKE A SPEAR

THE UNKNOWN AWAITS MY SOUL TO APPEAR

IF ONLY I COULD TELL THOSE AROUND ME WHO WAIT

MY LOVE I'D PROFESS WHILE ACCEPTING MY FATE

WE LIVE OUR LIVES THE BEST THAT WE CAN

BUT OUR FATE IS DECIDED BY OTHER THAN MAN

FREEDOM AWAITS BEYOND THE BRIGHT LIGHT

I FEEL THE WARMTH NOW AND
KNOW THAT IT'S RIGHT

I MUST GO BEYOND AND ABOVE, BUT WILL ALWAYS BE A PART OF THE ONES WHO I LOVE!!

Dcw 1984

Today we are here. Tomorrow we are gone. Life is too short to make everyone wrong. All strangers are friends when peace is our goal. All Strangers are enemies when Darkness is in our SOUL!

2003, The Columbia Shuttle Crew also met with disaster. They are forever Heros as well.

THANK YOU! MAHALO! DHANYAVAAD! A SHAYNEM DANK! SHUKRAN!

William McCool, Commander, "From our orbital vantage point, we observe the Earth without borders, full of peace, beauty and magnificence. And we pray that humanity as a whole can

imagine a borderless world as we see it, and strive to live as one in peace."

Laurel Clark, "We're incredibly lucky to be able to be working where we are up above the Earth and being able to see our Planet from that vantage point.

Ilan Ramon, "I believe that to be in space, to look at Earth from space, and to be able to contribute to Human Life so much, must be great".

Michael Anderson, "Along the way, he became a role model, especially for his two daughters and for the many children he spoke to in schools. He said, "What ever you want in life, you are in training for it now!"

Kaplan Chawla, MS "I think inspiration, and tied with it is motivation. "It is easy for me to be motivated and inspired by seeing somebody who just goes all out to do something. "She always wanted to reach the stars,"

David Brown, MS "Whatever I can do to contribute to Science to improve Science, I think is really great."

Rick Husband, "It was the achievement of a lifelong Dream and a Goal!

EULOGY

TO THE 2004 TSUNAMI VICTIMS AND SURVIVORS

This disaster was not a choice, but an act of GOD for whatever reason.

Death caused by Forces of Nature leaves no one to blame. We are left with Pain and Suffering. The World needs time to overcome the trauma to our Souls and our Earth. GOD has gotten our attention again. How many will hear the message that Life is too short for Should.

The extent of loss and devastation caused by the Tsunami is at a magnitude which has not been seen before. Humanity as a whole is suffering. The number of innocent Men, Women, and Children taken is profound. The Meek have taken a huge blow.

Believers in reincarnation might say, "Their individual Souls were many ages old and they have evolved to a point that they deserve to be at the side of our God (Buddha, Jesus, Mohammed, Allah, Valhalla, Ganesha, Moses, David, Universal Power) whatever you choose to call GOD."

Christians would say, "The Lord works in mysterious ways and never gives you something you can't handle." The Free Will, The Choice, is how we choose to handle the pain and help others handle their pain while they go forward towards the Betterment of Man.

New Age People would say, "Their collective energy will stimulate the Earth's vibration toward Love and Understanding of One and other. Let's Have Peace.

Believers in nothing would say, "170,000 People died."

To lose so many Innocent Souls in one fell swoop is cause for us remaining to reevaluate our daily Lives in order to be worthy of being left behind. Don't let a day go by without telling your Loved Ones how much you care.

God Bless Us with GRACE throughout the rest of our lives! God Bless those who are gone. May all those left behind forgive those who left the Planet with a Should on their last breath. Do not use this tragedy as an excuse to not carry on. All who have survived have been given the gift of Life again. Live a good compassionate life in Honor of those who have passed.

Let Us forgive ourselves for the Shoulds that crossed our minds after the Tsunami. There is no blame here. There is only room for doing. Let Us not get caught with a Should on our last breath.

At the time of this tragedy I was living in Southern California, where the sky is often obscured by clouds or smog. I wonder if anyone in Hawaii noticed any strange and beautiful events happening in the sky on the day of the tragedy or any days following. I choose to believe that all of the Innocent Humans that passed are with God.

I know the feeling of loss is Universal! Even the believers in nothing, must have felt something Only an individual truly disconnected from the Human Race all together could have gone untouched by this tragedy. Nature can restore its beauty in a matter of months. It can take some Humans a life time before they feel the beauty again. Free Will means Choice. We are in control. TAKE CONTROL OF YOUR FEELINGS AND DIRECT THEM TOWARD GOOD AND NOT EVIL.

The message was the same 27 years ago. Life is too short for should! Make Peace with yourself and each other before your time comes. A journey toward darkness will only bring more darkness. A journey toward the light brings joy and the peace of mind promised to all who have faith in GOODNESS.

LAMENT: 2005

TO THE 2005 HURRICANE KATRINA
VICTIMS AND SURVIVORS

This disaster was not a choice, but an act of God for whatever reason. Death caused by Forces of Nature leave no one to blame. We have nothing to do but reiterate the message we receive over and over again.

We are left with pain and suffering. The world needs time to overcome the trauma to our Souls and our Earth. GOD has gotten our attention again. How many will hear the message that, "Life is too Short for Should."

The loss of even one life is cause for all to mourn. In this case we are all mourning the individual loss of life as well as the collective loss of tradition, history, the feeling of security, and the faith that our systems are adequate.

Because of the technology along with the ability to communicate with each other through multimedia and the early warning system of this part of the world tens of thousands of lives were saved. Many people were able to get out of harm's way. Without cooperation many, many more lives would have been lost. Our systems will continue to get better!!!

The distinction between economic condition, religion, ethnicity, geographic location, sexual orientation, animal, mineral, and plant life is thrown away during a natural disaster. In a Should free world these variables would not be treated as a negative or a positive. They would be treated as an IS. All life is precious. Thank God for what IS.

Life is supposed to be positive, healthy, wealthy, wise and happy "With Malice towards None." Watching children play during a disaster reveals one of our basic human mechanisms! Coping with a situation, Children endure! Somewhere along the way adults forget how.

The Gulf Coast of Louisiana, Mississippi, and Alabama is now in need of an outpouring of love from the rest of the world. Love is the greatest healer on Earth. We combine love, money, faith, compassion, and hard work to create the brick and mortar necessary to build a strong foundation for new life.

The innocent men, women, children and animals that lost their life in this disaster are truly, now with God. Let us celebrate their lives by remembering them in a positive, nurturing and caring way. Let the grace of their existence fill the spirit of the Gulf and help mend the broken hearts of their loved ones. The life of those who suffered and survived is harder to understand then that of the loved ones who have passed. Once the choice to live is made we must "Keep On, Keeping On."

The sound of "Should" on the lips of survivors can be deafening. The number of "Shoulds" on the last breathe of the dying remain unheard. They will only be felt.

"Shoulds, Don't Count!!" All that is left is to do!! Our goal as humans is not to leave this planet with a should on our last breathe. Children are angels from God. They return directly to him without knowing a Should.

God Bless us with Grace throughout the rest of our lives! God Bless those who are gone. May all those left behind forgive those who left this plane with a should on their last breath. Do not use this tragedy as an excuse to not carry on. All who have survived have been given the blessing of life again. Live a good compassionate life in honor of those who have passed. You are not alone!!

RISKS

To laugh is to risk appearing the fool.

To cry is to risk appearing sentimental.

To reach out for another is to risk involvement.

To expose feelings is to risk exposing your true self.

To place your ideas, your dream before a crowd is to risk their loss.

To love is to risk not being loved in return.

To live is to risk dying.

To hope is to risk despair.

To try is to risk failure.

Anonymous?

Risks must be taken! The greatest hazard in life is to risk nothing. The person who risks nothing and does nothing has nothing. He has no Had. They may avoid suffering and sorrow, but they cannot learn, feel, change, grow, love and live a life worthy of them.

Persons deep in fear and hate are chained by their attitudes. They are a slave. They have forfeited their freedom. Only the person who risks giving and accepting love is truly free.

FEELINGS: AN INTRICATE ART

Feelings are hidden from all who might see

Feelings are hidden by you and by me

Sometimes we slip and reveal they are there

Those feelings of loneliness, pain, and despair

We fight to handle the fear that appears

We try not to remember the pain of past years

Some people cry and feel torment out loud

Some can express despair in a crowd

Some will hide loneliness with a smile or bright grin

Some will express deep pain from within

Some hide their feelings and won't shed a tear

But when out in a bar will cry in their beer!

Some will confess to being lonely sometime

Some will suggest feeling lonely is a crime!

Our hearts are too fragile for our minds to think clear

When loneliness, pain and despair do appear

To control these feelings and not fall apart

D. C. Williams

Can only be explained as an intricate art!

We study this art the best that we can

For not falling apart is at the heart of all man!

...DCW1985

CHAPTER 5

The Should Less Message Continues!

March 11, 2011 The Country of Japan was struck by the trifecta of all disasters. A horrific 8.9 magnitude earthquake, gave damage to 6 of the nation's nuclear energy power plants, and a 30 ft Tsunami created an event of Biblical proportions.

Over ten thousand people are missing from one village alone. The tsunami rose from the ocean depths and swept through the countryside causing buildings, cars, boats and debris to crash together as the turbulent, writhing, muddy water continued 6 miles inland.

With the technology of the 21st Century the world became, in real time, a collective eye-witness to the unbelievable devastation.

Japan is the 4th wealthiest Country in the World, the #1 authority on earthquake technology/preparedness and the #1 authority on nuclear energy power plant technology.

If Japan could not physically protect itself, what does that say for the rest of the world? The implications are staggering. It is time to connect with our Spiritual Self in order to find solutions.

The message is, no individual or Nation can protect itself from Mother Nature. All we can do is all we can do. Nature has a way of equalizing the playing field. Natural disasters remind us that we are only tenants and our landlord owns and operates this world at his will not ours.

There is no should here! Japan did everything humanly possible to protect their population from all of the above disasters. They built right, took preventative measures, and created the best earthquake/tsunami warning system in the world. They did everything right.

The only should that could appear, will be individual should. Without our human ability to protect ourselves from natural disasters we are left exposed. Our human short comings, jealousy, envy, fear, despair, regret and lack of faith, could start to appear. Pray for those who have gone with a should on their last breath. Remind the survivors, task is to live and grow!

The message is the same year after year. God keeps sending us messages and they get louder and louder for the entire world to hear!

This disaster was not a choice, but an act of God or course of nature, for whatever reason. Loss caused by force of nature leaves no one to blame. Although the redundancy can be maddening.

God has gotten our attention again. We are left with pain and suffering. The world needs time to overcome the trauma to our collective psyche and our Earth. How many more heard the message? "Life is too short for should!"

We must combine our love, money, faith, compassion, and hard work to create the metaphorical "Brick and Mortar" needed to rebuild this proud and revered nation.

The way Japan has rebuilt it's standing in the world since World War II is astounding. Former enemies have nothing but respect and admiration for the way its citizens have turned defeat, shame, pain, and anguish into positive production benefitting the world. "Leading from the front" is what they have managed to do.

My single mother of 3 was a teenager during WWII. Born in 1929 she lived through a time of world turmoil brought on by mans own choices. These devastating events were not natural. Nature had no involvement in what was taking place.

Death at the hands of a fellow human being "should never have happened!" As we know, "Shoulds don't count".

My mother, Christine passed away, June 30, 2010 at the age of 81 without a should on her last breath. Any animosity she may have had regarding the loss of her brother during World War II was gone. The hurt and anger toward her two ex-husbands was gone. Her beating herself up for not being more of the person she felt she could have been was gone. No should to be found on her last breath, only loving messages for her children, grand children, and great grand children.

Mother/Grandma Chris left an individual handwritten paragraph exclusive to each of her beloved grandchildren letting them know what special individuals they are and how they were and are always loved. Statements letting them know that she is well with her God and not to feel bad for her. As a giver, and a grandmother, her desire to comfort her loved ones at the time of her passing and not allow them to be left with a should on their mind or she leave with a should on her last breath, was extremely important to her. Peace and Love, taught and passed on insures a potential for a good life for generations to come. Changing a violent paradigm, to a peaceful one is Heaven.

Givers gain and Takers lose.

Mother was successful and never truly knew it. Many people have breathed easier because she lived. Not a bad testament, for a woman who became a mother at age 16.

"Do today, what you are willing to live with or take with you into infinity."

May 1, 2011, just months after my mother's passing, Osama Bin Laden, the world's most notorious taker, died with a litany of should on his last breath. He lived his life incessantly shoulding on others, "They should, you should, he, she and it should, the West Should, Muslims

should, non-believers should, Spain should, Britain should, US should, Shah should, Jews should, the Sheik should, all women and children should, believers should believe only my way, the World as a whole "should" believe as I do or it must be destroyed."

It was only fitting that our President, who represents all the people of the United States and its territories, give the final authority to capture and deal with our public enemy #1 at the time, Osama Bin Laden.

This President is a testament of what America is about. We have bi-racial Americans, Midwestern, White, Christian and African Americans. We have Black, Muslim, Buddhist, Catholic, Jewish, Hindu, Lutheran, Jehovah's Witness, Baha'i, Mormon, Shiite, Asian, Mexican, South American, Samoan, Tongan, Puerto Rican, Cuban, Russian, British, Australian, Indian, Canadian, Persian, Egyptian, Irish, Chinese, Japanese, Mexican, Cowboy, French, Spanish and probably Universal Alien Americans. America is diverse! A Country embraced and supported by the Constitution that took all humanity into consideration when it was created.

Our Presidents are not elected for their religious or ethnic backgrounds. They are duly elected individuals who are sworn into office and become the Commander-in-Chief of our military, the leader of the free world, and the duly elected head of all the people of the United States for four years. We then re-evaluate the President's contribution to our well being and either re-elect them for another four years or they are discharged and a new President is elected.

When our President dispatched Osama bin Laden over half of the World rejoiced, while the other half pondered the meaning of his death.

We are now in a Post Bin Laden era. Can we, as the human race find a way to use our free will and co-exist on this tiny planet?

My Choice is to re-establish our pre-Bin Laden way of perceiving success:

To laugh often

To gain the respect of intelligent people and the affection of Children

To earn the appreciation of honest critics and endure the Betrayal of fake friendship

To appreciate beauty

To find the best in others

To help improve the Human Condition

To know even one life has breathed easier because we have lived –Ralph Waldo Emerson

IF I HAD IT TO DO OVER...

By Nadine Stahr (Age 85)

Louisville, Kentucky

If I had my life to live over again, I'd make more mistakes next time. I would relax. I would limber up. I would be sillier than I've been on this trip. I know of very few things I would take seriously. I would worry less about what others thought of me and I would accept myself as I am. I would climb more mountains, swim more rivers and watch more sunsets. I would eat more ice cream and fewer beans. Would watch less TV and have more picnics.

I would have only actual troubles and very few imaginary ones. I would feel sad, not depressed. I would be concerned, not anxious. I would be annoyed, not angry. I would regret my mistakes but not spend a lot of time feeling guilty about them.

I would tell more people I liked them. I would touch my friends. I would forgive others for being human and I would hold no grudges.

I would grow with more children and listen to more old people. I would go after what I wanted without believing that I needed it. I wouldn't place such a great value on money.

You see, I'm one of those people who lived cautiously, sensibly, sanely, hour after hour, day after day. Oh, I've had my moments and if I had it to do over again, I'd have a lot more of them. In fact, I'd have nothing else – just moments, one after another, instead of living so many years ahead of each day. I have been one of those people who never went anywhere without a thermometer, a hot water bottle, a gargle, a raincoat and a parachute.

If I had it to do over again. I would go more places, do more things and travel lighter. I would plant more seeds and make the world more beautiful. I would express my feelings of love without fear.

If I had my life to live over, I would start barefooted earlier in the spring and stay that way later in the fall. I would play hooky more. I wouldn't make such good grades except by accident. I would ride on more merry-go-rounds. I'd pick more daisies and I would smile because I would be living free.

December of 2012 was lauded as "The End of the World as we know it"," based on the last day of the MAYAN CALENDER.

Instead of an end to the physical sphere we call Earth, an end did occur, but in the guise of a profound message delivered in the harshest of ways.

Just days before Christmas, the end did come to 26 gentle and defenseless souls at the hands of a 20 year old man. He used his free will and chose to destroy all that was beautiful and good around him. This evil doer stole the lives of 26 beautifully, wonderful people; 20 adorable Children and six of the caring, loving adults charged with their well being. The selfless courage, of the adults in defense of the children, is inspirational. Certainty has been shattered, but love will prevail with inter human support.

The total lack of compassion and thought for human life was apparent in this young man. He willfully took the lives of the innocent. He not only took the lives of those at Sandy Hook School, he also took the life of his mother and himself. Another casualty is the community of New Town, Once thought to be one of the safest communities in the Country.

This was a preventable act, and not an act of nature. The world received another clear message and gruesome account of a long standing collective problem. There appears to be a common thread among such individuals who act out of anger, rage, aggression, depression and mental health symptoms. Throughout the past 27 years the perpetrators appear to be Predominantly Rogue Young men full of rage and anger.

Such acts as the killing in 2006 at Virginia Tech University, Columbine school before that, the theatre shootings in Aurora, the blowing up of a the Federal Building, the shooting of President Ronald Reagan, the killing of John Lennon, the Menendez brothers, the shooting of Senator Gifford in Arizona and the 911 attacks on the International Trade Center in this century alone, all have a familiar link.

All of the perpetrators were young men from affluent families where the father's were somewhat to hugely successful. These fathers seem to have been unable, or unwilling to provide their sons with the love and nurturing necessary to create a balanced and secure individual. Without the guidance of a mature, responsible and loving adult role model, takers are created. Warped thinking is allowed to fester to the point of committing their evil deeds. True fatherly love is needed.

The last Century, produced the mega evil, Adolph Hitler. It took the World working together to cure that evil.

We in the 21ˢᵗ Century are in a huge battle for the spirit and soul of humanity. With instant information, we are emboldened to experience each natural disaster, each Victory, and each evil act in real time. TV, Skype, Utube, Twitter, Face book, individual smart phones, I Pads and the internet are our windows.

In the days since January 29, 1986, we as a Nation and the World have been receiving messages of biblical proportion. Many of which were featured in these pages.

On that fateful day, in December 2012, when a young man took the lives of the innocent we were again faced with the silence of those who passed. Children, do not have Should in their lives and go directly to GOD.

The "Shoulds" are immediate for those left behind. "Shoulds, Never Count". The damage is done. The only thing left to do is learn, ingest the lesson and vow to be more thoughtful, aware and eager to find help or deterrents for those in need before the Should occurs. Positive action honors those who passed. Takers take and leave only turmoil in their wake. The essence of a loved one, forced to move on is never lost. Good can come from one's life, however short or long.

Future battles are for the mind and spirit of our children. "Children learn what they live". Mental hurts are unseen, thus harder to treat.

Everyone has a story. How that story evolves from a Had, to a Have, depends upon how it is nurtured or disarmed. How we learn to reinforce good experiences and void or disarm the bad will determine the fate of humanity. Shoulds keep getting in the way. Eliminate the Should and we as Humans may become the meek, yet allowing future generations to truly inherit the Earth.

"Let the gentle Souls of thoughs leaving, caress the Souls of thoughs arriving, in order to perpetuate a Should Free Life!" Monetary success can be easily measured, and when inline with a wondrous Soul, the benefit to all of mankind is apparent and as Simple" as a Walnut!

"Do unto others as you would have others do unto you". Let us have a Should Free Life! Aloha

WE MUST HAVE!
TO CREATE A HAD!!!

WE MUST DO!
TO END THE SHOULD!!!

LIFE IS NOW, DON'T WASTE IT!

CHAPTER 6

At Last A Should Free Year!

WHAT IF NO ONE SHOULD ON YOU FOR 1 YEAR?

WHAT IF YOU DIDN'T SHOULD ON ANYONE?

WHAT IF YOU DIDN'T SHOULD ON YOURSELF?

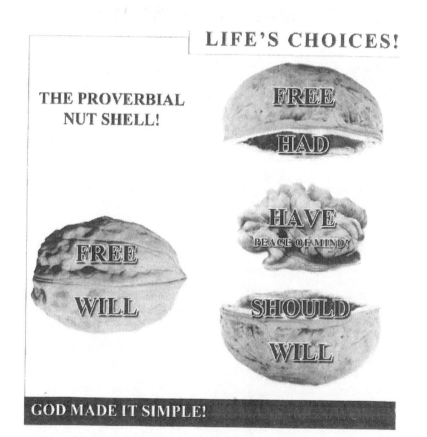

LIFE'S CHOICES!

THE PROVERBIAL NUT SHELL!

FREE
HAD

HAVE
PEACE OF MIND!

FREE
WILL

SHOULD
WILL

GOD MADE IT SIMPLE!

January

Sunday	Monday	Tuesday	Wednesday	Thursday	Friday	Saturday

February

Sunday	Monday	Tuesday	Wednesday	Thursday	Friday	Saturday

March

Sunday	Monday	Tuesday	Wednesday	Thursday	Friday	Saturday

April

Sunday	Monday	Tuesday	Wednesday	Thursday	Friday	Saturday

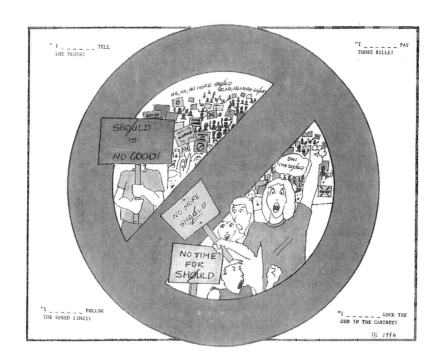

May

Sunday	Monday	Tuesday	Wednesday	Thursday	Friday	Saturday

June

Sunday	Monday	Tuesday	Wednesday	Thursday	Friday	Saturday

July

Sunday	Monday	Tuesday	Wednesday	Thursday	Friday	Saturday

PUT YOUR "SHOULDS" WHERE THEY BELONG!

August

Sunday	Monday	Tuesday	Wednesday	Thursday	Friday	Saturday

September

Sunday	Monday	Tuesday	Wednesday	Thursday	Friday	Saturday

October

Sunday	Monday	Tuesday	Wednesday	Thursday	Friday	Saturday

AVOID AN "AFTER-SHOULD".

November

Sunday	Monday	Tuesday	Wednesday	Thursday	Friday	Saturday

"UP / WITH PROACTIVE; DOWN \ WITH REACTIVE."

A LOVING YEAR OF PRICELESS BITS   COULD CREATE A CHRISTMAS MUCH LIKE THIS   WHERE ALL OF US ON PLANET EARTH   CAN SPEND MORE TIME ON JOY AND MIRTH.

December

Sunday	Monday	Tuesday	Wednesday	Thursday	Friday	Saturday

FYI: THE CHINESE ZODIAC

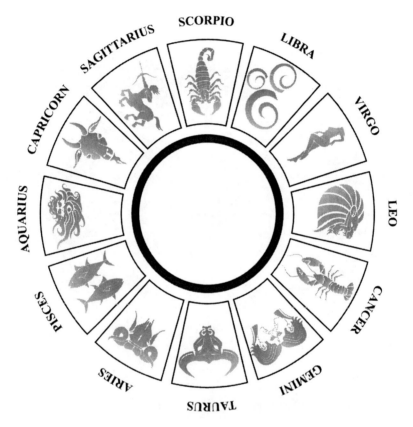

FYI: THE HOROSCOPE SIGNS

Q&A For Self Evaluation Answer At Your Own Free Will

WHAT IF NO ONE SHOULD ON YOU FOR 1 YEAR?

WHAT IF YOU DID'T SHOULD ON ANYONE?

WHAT IF YOU DIDN'T SHOULD ON YOURSELF?

How many people have you should on this year?

How many people should on you?

How many times have you should on yourself?

What are your favorite shoulds?

A.
B.
C.

How many times do you should a day?

How many times do you should a week?

What would your life be like without your shoulds?

How costly have your shoulds been in the last 6 months?

The Power Page

"I hear and I forget, I see and I remember. I do and I understand." Confucius

"Walk a mile in my shoes."-Unknown

"We are what we repeatedly do. Excellence then is not an act, but a habit."-Aristotle

"It is not because things are difficult that we do not dare; it is because we do not dare that they are difficult."-Seneca

"All truth passes through three stages. First, it is ridiculed. Second, it is violently opposed. Third, it is accepted as being self-evident." Arthur Schopenhauer

"I have always thought the actions of men are the best interpreters of their thoughts. -John Locke

"Pleasure in the job puts perfection in the work." Aristotle

"Paradigms are other people's habits passed on from generation to generation. Change a paradigm and you change a generation." -Bob Proctor

"We are Spiritual Beings, living a Human Experience" Dr. Wayne Dyer

"Today we are here! Tomorrow we are gone! Life is too short! To make everyone wrong!" DC Williams

CPSIA information can be obtained
at www.ICGtesting.com
Printed in the USA
FSOW02n1353270116
16260FS